FOR

I THINK YOU'D ENJOY THIS BOOK BECAUSE

FROM

PRINCIPLES FOR THE NEXT CENTURY OF WORK

Sense & Respond Press publishes short, beautiful, actionable books on topics related to innovation, digital transformation, product management, and design. Our readers are smart, busy, practical innovators. Our authors are experts working in the fields they write about.

The goal of every book in our series is to solve a real-world problem for our readers. Whether that be understanding a complex and emerging topic, or something as concrete (and difficult) as hiring innovation leaders, our books help working professionals get better at their jobs, quickly.

Jeff Gothelf & Josh Seiden

Series co-editors **Jeff Gothelf** and **Josh Seiden** wrote *Lean UX* (O'Reilly) and *Sense & Respond* (Harvard Business Review Press) together. They were co-founding principals of Neo Innovation (sold to Pivotal Labs) in New York City and helped build it into one of the most recognized brands in modern product strategy, development, and design. In 2017 they were short-listed for the Thinkers50 award for their contributions to innovation leadership. Learn more about Jeff and Josh at www.jeffgothelf.com and www.joshseiden.com.

MAKING PROGRESS

Issued in print and electronic formats.
ISBN 978-0-9994769-2-5 (paperback).
ISBN 978-0-9994769-3-2 (epub).

Editor: Victoria Olsen
Designer: Mimi O Chun
Interior typesetting: Jennifer Blais
Author photograph: Collaborative Fund

Published in the United States by Sense & Respond Press
www.senseandrespondpress.com

Printed and bound in the United States.
1 2 3 4   20 19 18 17

Ryan Jacoby

MAKING PROGRESS

The 7 Responsibilities of the
Innovation Leader

SENSE &
RESPOND
PRESS

PROGRESS, NOT JUST PROCESS

In the mid-1980s Gordon MacKenzie's employers
at Hallmark Cards wanted to move him from his
maverick position leading the Humor Workshop
to a more mainstream role within the corporate
bureaucracy. It was a promotion—of sorts—but
Gordon had misgivings. Would he be giving up his
freedom to innovate if he entered what he called "the
Big Grey Place"? His boss enticed him with an offer:
make up your own job title. So Gordon photocopied
(this was a long time ago) the definitions of the word
"paradox" and sent it to his boss with a note: "these
are the definitions of the word I would like as my job
title." He got the job of "Creative Paradox" and thus
began the intensely productive period he described
in his enduring business classic *Orbiting the Giant
Hairball*. In an interview he noted,

"As Creative Paradox, I fantasized that headquarters
was like New York City: conflicting endeavors, traffic,
lots of people, lots of neighborhoods—some safe, some
dangerous. I was a pushcart vendor, working on the
corner, selling without a license. My job was to bring
value to people on the street, all the while watching for
cops to turn up.

I became a liaison between the chaos of creativity
and the discipline of business. I had no job description
and a title that made no sense, but people started
coming to me with their ideas."

MacKenzie wasn't handed a relevant job description. If you are an
innovation leader I bet you weren't either. (I would also guess that
you haven't been allowed to come up with your job title!) So how
do you know where to start?

Like other functional roles—sales, marketing, operations—
the act of leading is usually different than doing the job itself. For
innovation, general leadership principles will help you, yet as an
innovation leader you have to walk the line between creativity and
consistency, new and old, exploration and execution, possibility
and probability. From the story, you see that MacKenzie, a creative
person at heart, is keenly aware of the business. He's not trying to
insulate himself from it; he's developing a productive relationship
with it so he could "bring value to people on the street," all while
avoiding the organizational tendency to stamp out change.

While there are many books, blog posts, and videos
online of people talking about what innovation is or proposing
a given innovation process, none that I've seen effectively
addresses innovation leaders and leadership directly. If
you're that innovation leader, this book is a tactical guide
for you. I've written it for the person charged with leading

innovation, regardless of the product or domain, no matter the organizational structure you've inherited or are meant to create, no matter the process you've adopted or want to adopt, whether you work in a brand-new start up or a Fortune 500 corporation. It's for managers and consultants, design directors and chief innovation officers, board members, CEOs, and recruiters. It will give you a framework for doing the job of "innovation leader" when the pressure to solve big problems feels bigger than ever and when your job is to lead a portfolio of projects and efforts, not just one.

SO, WHAT'S THE JOB?

Your job, first and foremost, is to **make progress**.

Progress means helping your organization expand its impact by better understanding and serving customers and by launching better products and services people value. Progress moves your organization forward productively—in a changing environment full of uncertainty. Making progress on innovation builds credibility for you and your team, which leads to more support and more resources, which in turn leads to more progress. Think of it this way:

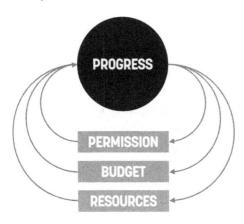

That's probably not on your LinkedIn page or on the job description you've been handed. And you can't make progress *eventually*: **you have to make progress this year, this month, this week**. So here are a set of responsibilities that, while not all easy to do, will help you in this unique job of leading innovation *now*:

» First, define what innovation progress means in
   your organization (#1),

Then you'll need to help your team get there:

» Set an innovation agenda (#2)
» Create and support teams that build (#3)
» Cultivate the ingredients for progress (#4)
» Give great feedback (#5)
» Inspire progress (#6)
» Reward progress (#7)

WHAT'S NOT YOUR JOB?
Process.

Don't get me wrong, innovation processes are important. Unfortunately they aren't sufficient for the job you need to do. Process tends to get most of the attention in the realm of innovation, but alone it's just not enough. Process is no substitute for innovation leadership.

If you're an innovation leader, **transformation isn't your job either**. I think of transformation as building the capability to do new things in new ways. It's developing the capability and capacity to innovate. Transformation helps you make progress, for sure. Your company might need digital, agile, customer-centricity, or other types of capability and cultural transformation in order to grow, innovate, or even survive. If so, transformation would absolutely help you innovate. Yet it's not the same thing as making innovation happen. Know if your job is really about innovation or transformation.

THE GOOD NEWS ABOUT PROCESS

Having a process is great for getting started: it gives you a framework when you don't have one. (Where should we start? What should we do next? When are we done with this step?) If you're training new employees, having a process will help them get oriented. If you're reorganizing your team, having a process can jumpstart big changes and give people a safe way to proceed. A process can comfort sponsors and stakeholders with the feeling that things are happening.

Today there are many innovation processes, methods, ideas, steps, workshops, and project structures: Design Sprints, Design Thinking, Customer Discovery, Lean Startup, Lean Startup for the Enterprise, SCRUM, or Lean UX. I like to think of them as helping you do new things for the existing business and for building new businesses. The choice of which processes to use when is really important. As Jeff Gothelf, co-author of *Sense & Respond* and co-founder of this press, says, process is often "hired for the wrong reasons"— to increase speed, for example, rather than increase impact or effectiveness. The books, courses, consultants, workshops, and conferences that can help you navigate those choices are plentiful and useful, but that's not what I'm focused on in this book. (What else this book won't do: it won't help you find budget or resources for your projects and it won't defend "innovation" as a term or idea.)

THE BAD NEWS ABOUT PROCESS

Process doesn't align people who aren't part of the day-to-day operations. Process can't decide which projects to start and which to stop. It can't sense as well as a leader can when something's going wrong within a team. And while a process might have a "learning" step, it can't remember for you or encourage a team to really learn from what they're doing. A single process, mechanically followed, is by definition not very agile or responsive. It doesn't set up well for change.

If your team doesn't have a process and they need something, pick one up quickly and start using it. But don't make your job about instituting that process. Be careful when team members, who are most familiar with one particular process, begin to focus on the process more than progress. No matter which process you use, it should never become the end in itself.

Okay, let's get to it.

Note: This book is designed for browsing. You don't need to read it straight through from front to back to benefit from these principles. Feel free to skim and return later or jump ahead. Look to the end of sections for activities and reflections on your own progress along the way.

RESPONSIBILITY 1: DEFINE INNOVATION PROGRESS

If making progress happen is your job, determining what progress to make is the first step. You might think, "of course we know what progress means around here," but don't skip this step. It buys credibility, it's framed in terms of impact, and it sets the stage for the work you'll do (and won't do).

If you meet your CEO in the elevator this is how you'll describe what you're working on: not "seven innovation projects," but **how your work will impact *your* company and *your* customers in *your* markets**, both new and old. A focus on making progress goes beyond the C-suite too. In *The Progress Principle*, Harvard Business School professor Teresa Amabile demonstrates that, whether for innovation or not, rewarding work comes from making progress. Employees are motivated by getting things done.

As a consultant, I've seen firsthand that innovation progress means something different at every company. Even when companies are in the same category, industry, or market, meaningful progress can be and ought to be defined differently. Even when customers overlap, the core assumptions that an organization holds, how they operate, the targets they use to measure themselves, and the timeframe that it takes to get new things launched can vary wildly. Ford and Uber both help people move from place to place, but how they've done it to date and how they might want to do it in the future are different. Goals and aspirations aside, every company has a track record that suggests what innovation progress has meant in practice.

START BUILDING CREDIBILITY

Tackling the big metrics is part of the innovation leader's job. Making progress against those metrics develops credibility and earns you more resources and responsibility. Often innovation gets saddled with a reputation for dreaming more than doing, and justly so. As Renn Turiano, who has led design and product at Amazon and NBC Universal told me, "First, you must demonstrate that you're not frivolous."

As an innovation leader, you need to be both informed and specific about mission and goals, the organization's track record, and market considerations even as they change and evolve.

You'll need to embrace the language of business and strategy in addition to the more traditional creative innovation disciplines of design, marketing, engineering, and technology. If you "know the numbers" as well as or better than anyone else in the room that will do wonders for your credibility.

CONNECT INNOVATION ACTIVITIES TO BUSINESS OUTCOMES

Innovation increases customer impact and, as a result, organizational impact. Expectations seldom match reality, or as Larry Selden and Ian MacMillan have written:

> "For many companies, there's a huge difference between what's in their business plans and the market's expectations for growth.... This growth gap, as we call it, springs from the fact that companies are pouring money into their insular R&D labs instead of working to understand what the customer wants and then using that understanding to drive innovation."

It's not just revenue or profit goals. The same goes for customers. At minimum, seek to understand the target and actual numbers of customers, growth rates, customer acquisition costs, and segment profitability (or lifetime value, LTV). If there aren't clear priorities for focus and improvement, work alongside sales and marketing leaders to create them.

Making progress means overcoming the **growth gap** and **customer gaps** you've identified. To be successful, you need to realistically assess the time, cooperation, and resources it will take to close those gaps. Look back at past projects and uncover what accelerated growth and what limited it. Beware of the "we're looking for $100M ideas" people in your organization, especially if that statement isn't informed by what the organization has been capable of creating in the past. When I hear those statements, I have a tendency to dismiss them as uninformed bluster or misplaced "big, hairy audacious goals."

One rule of thumb comes to me from Rita Gunther McGrath. When she talks about forecasting growth, she challenges business leaders to ask: what would need to be true to grow operating profit by 10%? For example, if your company had $50M in operating profits last year, what would have to be true to create $5M in incremental profit through new products, services, or an emerging new business?

UNDERSTAND THE PACE OF PROGRESS AND ACTIVELY MANAGE THE THROTTLE

You need to understand "how fast is fast?" A client at a global organization once told me that she had a team that was in "year four of a pilot." If it's year four, it's hard to imagine that it's a pilot and I certainly don't believe that the innovation leader should be responsible for it at that stage. As an innovation leader, you might be constrained by an existing route to market or you might be challenging yourselves to create new pathways to get things launched.

Develop a perspective on the appropriate phase lengths for projects all the way to launch. Rarely do I find organizations that want to move more slowly, but that doesn't mean you should move recklessly forward either. Try to increase the pace by eliminating distractions and giving appropriate support and staging investment so you lower the cost of failure—without reducing the validity of what you're doing. Good answers are often better than fast answers. Adopting an Agile or Lean Startup process would let you take more swipes at a problem, but (again) don't let process (or speed) become an end in itself.

DON'T WAIT TO ASK "WHAT'S NEXT?"

Start every innovation project with the next step in mind. When I start a project with a client I pose these questions: If your innovation efforts were wildly successful in the next eighteen months, what would happen? How about six months? How would others in your organization know innovation was working? How would your customers know if innovation was working? That discussion allows us to design the right approach to keep moving new offerings forward. It's important to understand the end game. Doing so will help you develop relationships with people who can operate and scale your new offerings and give insight into what leads to great, scaled businesses.

Know the type of outcome you're looking to make. Not every type of launch is the same. Some new offerings suit your existing infrastructure. Others are far more risky because of a lack of technical capabilities or the maturity or competitiveness of a market. There are a handful of good innovation portfolio models out there, some of which are similar to one another. Rita Gunther McGrath has a great discussion about the different types of innovation options. Steve Blank has a great discussion about different types of markets that applies to existing companies as well as startups (see Citations). Get to know these frameworks for a more informed definition of progress.

ACTIVITIES

Define your growth gap.

» What growth is possible? What parts of the business might it come from? What contribution could innovation make?

Consider your market.

» Where might new customers come from? Who could be a competitor of yours tomorrow that isn't today?

Assess your assumptions and evidence.

» What fundamental assumptions do you and your organization have about growth?

» What do you know about your future growth plans with a great deal of confidence? What are you unsure about?

Consider your pace.

» When was the last new product or service introduction at your company? How long did it take from inception to launch? What happened to the product since? How typical was that process? What accelerated and what dampened its progress?

Plan your landing.

» Would your team take things through a pilot? Would you launch a new service and run it until you can transition to a more operational leader?

» Consider your metrics for progress. If you don't have any, create one or two.

RESPONSIBILITY 2: SET AN INNOVATION AGENDA

Once you know how you define and measure progress you'll want to **put together an innovation agenda that clearly articulates the future-critical challenges you will be working on as a team.** It's important to align on the customer problems, strategic opportunities, and big questions you have going into the project; like any good strategy, this should also point out what you're **not** doing.

If you fail to set your own agenda, you risk becoming the island of misfit problems—a place where everyone in the company dumps the random projects they don't know what to do with, the questions they can't answer, or whatever popped up as interesting at the last executive cocktail party or jet trip. That could land you in a process quagmire ("we're making the organization more agile") or reinforce a negative perception of innovation ("who knows what they're doing over there?").

An innovation agenda has at minimum three distinct components. To start, **articulate and share what you see as 1) the priority innovation problems, 2) customer groups, and 3) types of innovation to pursue.** Over time, you might elaborate on these by adding processes and organizational structures, but for now focus on these three elements (after all process does not equal progress).

An innovation agenda isn't a project list, as not everything on the agenda will have a project associated with it yet. Or you might have many different projects all addressing similar problems or customer groups. It pays to remember that *your* problems should be carefully crafted, not just inherited or taken on by default. You are not responsible for fixing every broken idea or addressing every existential threat that's dropped at your doorstep, just the ones you decide to prioritize.

Here are some principles and examples for the three crucial pieces of your agenda: defining the problem, identifying the customer, and articulating the type of innovation you'll prioritize.

ARTICULATE YOUR PRIORITY INNOVATION PROBLEMS

PRIORITY INNOVATION PROBLEMS

DEFINITION

» The high-impact challenges you're prioritizing for innovation as an organization. Prioritizing them means you're interested in developing new solutions and new models for solving these problems rather than improving, scaling, or operating what's been created.

DOs & DON'Ts

DOs

» Be specific
» Make sure they are customer-focused
» Position these for adoption ("problems", "opportunities," "big questions")
» Be wary of potential solutions posing as problems

DON'Ts

» Adopt problems where there is little room for innovation
» Take on problems that leave little room for progress
» Assume every problem has to be an existential one—many "small" problems can have a big impact

EXAMPLES

» An online food and grocery service: We want to help young professionals, consumed by work, get dinner on the table.
» An urban library: We want to educate people to become employable adults in today's and tomorrow's economy.
» A fitness company: We want to help busy people struggling with motivation to begin to integrate fitness into their everyday life.
» A technology company: We want to help homeowners use technology to make their homes more capable and comfortable.

ARTICULATE YOUR INNOVATION TARGET (PEOPLE, CUSTOMERS, CONSUMERS, ETC.)

PRIORITY CUSTOMERS, CONSUMERS, OR PEOPLE

DEFINITION

» These are the people, whether or not they're customers today, that you want to help and develop relationships with as an organization. You'll want insights and deep understanding into these people, how to serve them, and how to reach them.

DOs & DON'Ts

DOs

» Get beyond demographics to address situations, "jobs to be done," etc.

DON'Ts

» Forget suppliers in marketplace models

EXAMPLES

» An established financial services company: Recent graduates and those entering the workforce
» A financial services venture: Retirees and their families
» A nonprofit: Food-insecure people seeking pantry assistance

ARTICULATE THE TYPE OF OUTPUT YOU EXPECT TO CREATE AND LAUNCH

THE TYPES OF INNOVATION YOU'RE FOCUSED ON DELIVERING

DEFINITION

» This is what you'll "make" as a team and as an organization and which will be delivered to your customers through your mechanisms for reaching the market, such as:

- Services delivered through people interactions
- Digital services
- New brands and supporting interactions
- Core platform technology
- Adjustments and improvements to the existing business model
- Partnership service interactions
- New businesses and startups

DOs & DON'Ts

DOs

» Set yourself up to be successful

» Consider whether you're seeking incremental or revolutionary outcomes

DON'Ts

» Claim a type of innovation you're not likely to be able to deliver

EXAMPLES

» A global news organization: Digital subscription services on mobile and web

» A global hospitality and travel company: On- and off-property service interactions

» A CPG company: Whole new ventures that deliver incremental new revenue to our business

Once you've identified a problem—say, getting dinner on the table—**refine the statement to make it more usable, specific, and appropriate** to your organization. Whether you're a grocery company, a food manufacturer, a meal kit startup, or a recipe-based online site, get more specific about how you're going to go about solving the problem:

» Who are you targeting? Amateur foodies? Time-pressed professionals? Stay-at-home parents? Food-insecure rural residents?

» What makes their situation unique?

» What behaviors are already in place? What motivations do they have?

» Does their problem happen occasionally or all of the time?

Using some of those prompts, here are some other refinements of the "dinner on the table" problem:

» We want to help busy people get dinner on the table.

» We want to help busy parents with kids get dinner on the table so we can eat together as a family.

» We want to help food-insecure people in rural communities find emergency food assistance to feed their families.

» We want to help busy people, trying to be healthier, get dinner on the table and avoid the takeout/delivery guilt.

» We want to help young professionals, consumed by work, get dinner on the table (or desk) when they have to stay late at the office.

» We want to help couples, looking for meaningful time together, get dinner on the table while having fun together.

Defining customer problems can help shape the problem space, help you be clear about what you're not pursuing, and inspire drastically different potential solutions to prototype.

CUSTOMERS OR PROBLEMS? PROBLEMS OR CUSTOMERS?

Start with what you have. What if you don't know the customer's problems yet? That happens all the time. You'll find yourself interested in new types of customers or potential customers and will be searching for the type of problems that they need help with. For example, a financial services company I worked with knew that they were interested in the messy period of life when adult children need to get more involved in managing their aging parents' affairs. The problems and potential solutions in that phase of life were vast, with some being far more interesting to the company than others. In entrepreneurial settings, this is what Steve Blank and others describe as "customer discovery." Start by defining the areas where you have more certainty, experience, or conviction and let that guide you towards where to focus next.

FOCUS ON WHAT'S "NEW" AND WITHIN YOUR CONTROL

Focus on activities that lead to *new*: new customers, new offerings, new businesses. Unless you're in charge of innovation for the entire company, focus on the areas of the business where you're responsible for progress. Your team's core work should be different than what the rest of the business works on. That's important. There are other types of innovation, of course, that lead to operational efficiency, for example, but we're not focused on those here. It's very tough to do all types of innovation in one group, so if you are leading both types of activity for the time being, separate the groups.

No doubt there will be other innovators and innovation happening within the organization. That's a good thing. There will also be people interested in doing new innovative things who want to help you or who will be motivated to do things on their own. Also a good thing. Resist any urge to control those activities, especially in the beginning. Be generous with what you learn and what you're doing, while also staying focused on your own span of control.

You want to choose ambitious problems in line with the business goals you defined in Responsibility #1. Tread carefully here: I see lots of organizations and leaders declare they want to solve problems, reach customers, or make types of innovation they're not set up to make progress on either efficiently or effectively.

"DO YOU"

Craft an innovation agenda that's as **authentic** as it is ambitious, as probable as it is provocative. Chasing after problems that aren't core to your mission, your capabilities, and your sense of purpose is not likely to result in actual progress. It might happen, but you'd be getting even luckier than you already have to be.

I recently worked with the Knight Foundation to discover what innovation meant in urban libraries and assess the capability of major urban libraries to get there. As part of that work, I used the innovation agenda to help interview 30+ top U.S. library leaders. The Knight Foundation published this research online as "Developing Clarity: Innovating in Library Systems" (see the Citations at the end of the book).

Looking at the priority innovation problems across the entire field, the emphasis varied. Some library leaders wanted their innovation to focus on traditional library services and others wanted to fill what one respondent called "community deficits." The former wanted innovation projects to focus on access to education, knowledge, and literacy, which could reinvent how libraries do what they do. The latter wanted innovation projects to address civic problems, which could redefine the role of libraries in urban life. Both directions can and do make a lot of sense and likely make even more sense given the particulars of each library system. Embrace an agenda that makes sense and helps your organization grow.

SHARE YOUR AGENDA FREQUENTLY AND REVISIT IT OCCASIONALLY

A good agenda gets buy in from internal partners and supporters. This gets you budget and air cover. You avoid being the island of misfit problems and it helps with recruiting talented innovators and builders. With a solid definition of innovation progress and a prioritized and aligned innovation agenda, you avoid being "the team over there working on who knows what."

Developing an agenda might not be the absolute first step in your job—there's value in making progress first—but if you don't do a version of this within the first six to nine months (whether or not your bosses ask for it), it's a mistake.

Consider prototyping your agenda with colleagues, your team, partners, and allies within the organization. Think of it as a slow-growing, living document. I'd recommend revisiting it no less than every six months and whenever you start projects. Share it during hiring discussions and when you meet people throughout the organization (a test in its own right). Innovators love to know what big problems they're working on and by sharing yours, you can extract interested and interesting people (see Responsibility #3). The contents shouldn't change quickly; what you do with it should.

ACTIVITIES

Align on problem statements.

» What priority customer problems or business problems are you trying to solve?

» What problems should you be solving that have gotten less attention than they deserve?

» What type of customer do you think should be explored more? What customer problems or situations are less known than they should be?

Align on customer insights.

» Think about your current customers: What new things might you do for them? What are they getting elsewhere that they could get from you? How specific can you be about them and their problems?

» Think about the customers you want: Where are they today? Are they on the sidelines? Are they being served elsewhere?

RESPONSIBILITY 3: CREATE & SUPPORT TEAMS THAT BUILD

Like any leader, you'll need to build great teams and support them. Nothing new here! As teams go, innovation teams *are* unique though. **Innovation benefits from diversity, technical depth, and people with complementary process tendencies.** Brought together to solve a challenging problem for customers, such people leverage their differences in pursuit of new, big things. **Get beyond "cross-functional." Your team should be dedicated to building and learning.** You won't always get to choose your team members from the start, so you'll need to help people find new ways to work even as you actively bring people in or move people out of your group. Here are some ways to start.

EMBRACE THE BUILDERS

Find and support the "builders." Builders are people who have a track record of getting things into the world in some way, shape, or form—hopefully within your organization and hopefully in different environments. They'll be scrappy and entrepreneurial. They'll exhibit intense curiosity, value learning, and be willing to try things, getting feedback in any way they can. Builders aren't going to wait for you to tell them what to make and they're rarely going to show up with a single idea, hoping it's the right idea. They'll bring several ideas to the table, usually right from the start, even if they don't completely believe in each idea themselves.

Make sure you have people who are not only general builders, but also are capable of building the types of innovation you've prioritized (services, technology, channels, partnerships, marketing, etc.). Then once you've got them, use them well: if you've got designers and builders sitting around waiting for strategy to happen, you're going to be dealing with decreased motivation (and moonlighting employees). Frank Hauser's *Notes on Directing* is a classic compendium of advice for theater directors working with actors and crew. Written as a series of brief aphorisms—like *"Don't expect to have all the answers"* and *"Assume that everyone is in a permanent state of catatonic terror,"* the book is filled with tips that are equally useful for anyone working in creative collaborations. One such pithy piece of advice is *"Never keep the talent waiting."*

DIVERSIFY AND BALANCE TEAMS

Create teams that can complement each other as they make progress. Some people love generating ideas, but are less energized when executing them. Other people love planning and research, but get anxious committing to a direction. It's your job to find the right mix of attitudes and tendencies on your teams—and correct as you go along.

A common problem I've seen is a team weighted to one extreme or the other: teams that keep spinning their wheels (moving Post-its and generating ideas without getting to concrete design) or teams that jump the gun and start designing in excruciating detail the first idea that materializes. Of course sometimes the first idea *is* the right idea and sometimes we really don't know enough about the customer. That doesn't mean the team is all aligned to that perspective though. Use a process of exploration and execution to move quickly through to better ideas. Too much exploring and too much execution can be counterproductive. You need a balance of insight and action, prototyping and strategy.

GET DEDICATED

Find people able to commit the time and energy to each project. A favorite professor of mine and one of the founding faculty at the Stanford d.school, Jim Patell, was once teaching a class about wait times and utilization in queues. A classmate asked him, "What's a good utilization number?" Jim, always a character, replied "This is the point when most professors say 'It depends.' I won't do that. If you have 85% utilization you're doing great and come see me." Channeling Jim, your team members should be able to commit six uninterrupted hours four times a week or they're off the project.

It's more important for your team to be dedicated than to be "cross-functional." I'd rather work with a balanced, diverse three-person team who are "all in" than fifteen people who cover every division of the company but can never find time to really do the hard work. While it's good to get operators and scalers involved in the process, there are plenty of mechanisms to get them involved, exposed, and bought in if they can't be dedicated (such as having them participate in prototyping or piloting).

OWN THE WHOLE PROBLEM

Insist that team members own the "whole problem." In my experience, these teams are more successful and build better innovation. For innovation, the whole problem is

» Finding customer problems

» Discovering and distilling customer insights

» Prototyping and getting feedback on ideas through experimentation

» Designing winning solutions and value propositions

» Creating business model opportunities and implications

» Getting new offerings and businesses launched

All team members should ideally be proficient, and at least, interested in all of these aspects of the problem. Otherwise you're missing the true value of the multidisciplinary approach. This is where process comes in—a good process can get team members exposed and involved in the whole problem. As *The New York Times* was experimenting with building its approach to digital product development, they learned that a good initial team would be composed of a product person, a design person, a technologist, and an editor (somewhat unique to news organizations, but you could imagine a medical professional, a teacher, etc.), with support from market research. Despite their different backgrounds, everyone was still expected to care about the customer, the solution, the business model, and the importance of everyone else's technical domain.

As you watch your team interact notice their patterns so you can adjust for imbalances. Productive disagreement is fine—in fact, you want diversity of opinions as well as diversity in general—but you want your whole team to be invested in collaborating and owning the whole problem. If there's someone on your team with valuable expertise that's not being utilized, that's a problem. As Hauser noted, you don't keep the talent waiting. Team members who are under-utilized, under-appreciated, or under-heard will disengage—or worse, sabotage the project.

FREE THEM UP TO DO THE WORK

You have to help your team members stay focused on solving the problem. Innovation is hard. Innovation is really hard if a significant portion of a team's time is focused on creating presentations to get stakeholders up to speed on what's happening. Sharing what they've seen, what they're trying, what they're learning, and what they're building is important. But don't let reporting become an end in itself. As a leader, you should help shoulder the burden of status reports and executive updates. Consider encouraging teams to use "stand ups," especially with extended teams. In a stand up, the whole meeting lasts fifteen minutes, with each person simply sharing progress made yesterday and progress to be made today. (For more on feedback, see Responsibility #5).

SET THE PACE

Use deadlines creatively to keep things pushing forward. A trick I like to use with new clients is to schedule customer feedback sessions as soon as a week or two into working together. When we schedule the sessions, we don't have anything to show yet. Knowing that customers are on the calendar gets the team moving, expressing their hunches as prototypes, and helps to remove any resistance to spending time with customers. This is what the Lean Startup and customer discovery people are doing when they force workshop participants to "get out of the building." The same type of thinking can be useful later in a project. Agile software development offers lots of techniques and methods for assessing work and setting schedules, but not all innovation is software-based or solely software, so you have to find other ways to set deadlines.

When we were transitioning from the early stages of defining what would become NYT Cooking, *The New York Times* team had to decide what interactions and features would go into the first pilot. Instead of debating the interactions and features, we set a date in early December and used that to help decide which features were most important to test our assumptions and that we'd be able to execute reasonably well. When asked by the team why we chose this date, I said we'd want to be done with development by Thanksgiving and run the initial pilot in early December before the holiday season picked up. No real reason other than to *keep moving*.

ACTIVITIES

» Identify the builders in your organization. How can you get them involved on your projects? How do you make it easy for them to build?

» Think about the balance of the team. Do you have a good mix of insight and action? Strategy and execution?

» If you created a deadline, or a moment for feedback, to get a team moving again, what would it be?

RESPONSIBILITY 4: CULTIVATE THE INGREDIENTS FOR PROGRESS

If you've read these sections in order you already know the importance of a **dedicated, balanced team** and **an innovation agenda that defines the right problem statement and focuses on customer insights.** Those are just some of the requirements for successful innovation. **The other ingredients for progress are strategic questions, assumptions, options, and evidence.**

These ingredients are the life-blood of progress. Your job is make sure that you create and share these ingredients. They are essential for any given project, but they also have staying power. It's likely that you'll be focused on certain customer problems and certain customers for a long time—cataloging what you know, what you've seen, and what you believe about them should be important. Too often, organizations go on to developing the next solution, but they don't stop to realize that some customers or customer problems will stay the same and you can still build on earlier insights. If developed, validated, and shared independently of any particular project or solution, these ingredients are a "gift that keeps on giving." (You'll notice what's *not* on this list: ideas and solutions. Those emerge *from* the ingredients and evolve with technology and time.)

PROBLEM STATEMENTS FOCUS, MOTIVATE, AND DIRECT

It's become cliché, perhaps, but it's still important to "fall in love with the problem, not the solution." In the discussion of innovation agendas in Responsibility #2, I shared problem statements from project work I've done. Don't hurry through finding a problem statement, but don't agonize over it either. Throw something out there and start to refine it. Even the wrong problem, so to speak, can get you started on discovering the right one. If you're stuck, start exploring assumptions you have about the basic motivations and behaviors of customers. A good definition of product design comes from the designer Keenan Cummings: "recognizing patterns of human behavior, discovering the motivations and impulses that drive those patterns, [and then] creating [offerings] that improve or elevate the output of those behaviors." Understanding those patterns of behavior, motivations, and opportunities get you well on your way to defining the problem.

CUSTOMER INSIGHTS INSPIRE SOLUTIONS, VALUE PROPOSITIONS, AND DESIGN

Don't overlook or take for granted the power of true, deep customer insight. We already talked about customer insights as part of your agenda in Responsibility #2. Despite the lip service to customer-centricity, most organizations neglect them. You have to change that. So how will you recognize great customer insights? Definitions vary, but I like one used at Diageo, the global beverage company: "penetrating discoveries that unlock growth." You should be pushing your teams to distill clear and actionable insights in their projects, sharing what you've seen with whomever will listen.

Informed perspectives are better than desk-assembled stories you *hope* are true. While personas, especially if used correctly, can help get you beyond aggregate data and faceless demographics, real customer stories can only come from real customer interactions and hopefully contain feedback on your assumptions captured through prototypes and experiments. Then you have to translate your insights into action. Strategic questions and assumptions will help you do that.

STRATEGIC QUESTIONS GUIDE DISCOVERY

Embrace the questions you have and treat each one with respect. A question is often as important or as pressing as a customer problem or other type of assumption. A question is strategic if it has an answer that will make or break the solution or validate or invalidate an assumption. We discuss different examples below, but strategic questions might be as far-reaching as: How are tomorrow's customers different and similar to those today? What regulatory changes might impact our potential solutions? They also might be "small," yet important like: What does "fun" mean in the kitchen, when cooking a meal? How much variety in recipes is exciting and how much becomes too taxing?

Not every question is answered the same way, however. I like to draw a distinction between questions where the answers are *knowable* and questions where the answers are *discoverable*. *Knowable* answers can be looked up: there's an answer that's already out there and you just have to find it. *Discoverable* answers are ones you have to figure out through prototyping and experimentation. This difference can help you direct a team's research more productively—but you'll need to make sure they ask both kinds of questions.

Imagine for a second that you were interested in creating a new financial services offering for young people, helping them establish themselves on a path to lifelong financial wellness. What follows is a list of some of the strategic questions you could ask and whether they are mostly knowable, mostly discoverable, or an interesting hybrid. The last column shows how we might get more insight or evidence of the "right" answer. It's better to use prototyping to accelerate customer research and to test assumptions quickly, so whenever you see a hybrid question expect to use low-fidelity prototypes to explore the answer.

NEW FINANCIAL SERVICES OFFERING DISCOVERY

QUESTION	ANSWER TYPE	INSIGHT SOURCES
» What's the current state and cutting edge of (financial) advice? What new models, experiences, and trends should inspire us?	» Mostly knowable	» Direct usage » Trends » Landscape scans » Ask advanced users
» How many new college graduates will be in a position to start saving within the first three years of graduation?	» Knowable	» Start with survey and employment data » Look for evidence of account creation and 401K opt in
» What's the right balance of tailored, in-person advice and expert recommendations?	» Discoverable	» Prototype mix, using the same recommendations to isolate the effect of the mix
» What's the role of experts? Family members? Friends?	» Hybrid	» Mix customer research with prompts and early prototypes
» What, if anything, are people using today to meet their financial needs? What services are growing? Waning?	» Hybrid	» Mix customer research with prompts and early prototypes

ASSUMPTIONS FRAME RISK AND DIRECT EXPERIMENTATION

Look for, listen for, and clearly articulate your assumptions. Assumptions are at the heart of the creative process, at least in business. Russell Ackoff, one of the great managerial and "systems" academics, was a wise and acerbic observer of organizations. He wrote in the 1970s and 1980s, but his observations are still apt. Ackoff believed that creativity starts with breaking an assumption:

> "The creative act is always an act in which you identify an assumption that you have made which prevents you from seeing alternatives, removing that assumption, and exploring the consequences."

We all bring hunches to an innovation project so it's important to get those out and shared amongst the team. At the beginning of projects, the first thing to do is catalog your collective hunches and assumptions about the problem, the customer, the product, the market, the business, etc. As the project progresses, update those assumptions and hunches. Turn some of these hunches into more explicit hypotheses, testing them with prototypes and experiments.

Getting clear about these assumptions not only sparks creativity, but also reminds you what you're doing and why you're doing it. Do you ever find yourself in the middle of a project update feeling like you can't remember what you set out to do or why it was important? You're not alone. In a study, Ackoff estimated the "half life" of a managerial assumption as approximately six weeks. Said differently, half the managers in an organization will forget their core assumptions within six weeks. That's one reason I like to cap project phases with clients to around four-to-six weeks. Any longer and extended team members start to forget what they're doing and why they wanted to do it.

CREATE DISTINCT STRATEGIC OPTIONS

Keep ideas as separate as you can, for as long as you can. In a financial sense, innovation is about creating so-called "strategic options." A strategic option, like holding a lease on an undrilled oil field, gives you a choice to pursue a direction now or in the future. Usually it takes money to "exercise" an option (through further design, implementation) or you might be able to sell the option to someone else (intellectual property). An option is inherently valuable, even if you don't exercise it, as long as you aren't spending a ton of time or money to keep it viable and it, in fact, remains viable.

Within and across teams, you should strive to cultivate distinct solution alternatives that address the customer problem and insights you've seen. There are lots of different techniques and frameworks for exploring and documenting solutions, but don't let the frameworks—which are often good at helping you document your best-guess option right now—get in the way of creating different options.

Keep in mind that big problems don't always need big solutions. For example, remember when grocery stores started turning the scanner display towards the customer? That really helped solve a problem of the hassle and time of price checks with clerks. It also built trust with customers. Ask yourself, what could you do about your problem in a couple of weeks of design time and have in the market right away that could make a difference?

Use prototyping to get feedback and evidence on multiple options early in your process to avoid spending too much cost, time, and resources (in software development, for example). At my consulting company, I like to think of this as building options and deciding what to keep, rather than spending an inordinate amount of time and resources deciding what one option to build. We strive to take six or seven interesting provocations with us out into the field right from the start. Editing, especially when it's informed by evidence, feels *great* and is a good way to work with colleagues and sponsors to align on what you will do.

CAPTURE EVIDENCE AND LEARNING

As an innovation leader, you should make sure that the evidence is both clear and well-communicated. I believe strongly in the value of instincts and hunches and beliefs, especially at the beginning of a project. To get incremental support, there are all kinds of evidence that you can draw on even before sales and growth numbers: prototype feedback, data from experiments and campaigns, stories from customers, stories from frontline staff, firsthand experiences, knowledge gleaned from past projects. Once you're in the market the best evidence is usage, growth, customer recommendations, and customer feedback. Evidence aligns team members and helps avoid the "this is the first time we've tried this" fallacy.

You might articulate a set of customer insights and get vigorous nodding along with the response that "we know this" or "we didn't need to do a project to find this out." Um, maybe. But where's the evidence? That's when you need validated learning. Build prototypes that target the riskiest assumptions and tackle the most important discoverable questions, then share them. A prototype that hasn't been shared really isn't a prototype in my book.

SHARING IS A FORM OF DOING

Test how well you and the rest of the organization knows something by sharing it. The final stage of "knowing" anything is do something with it. First, get those new offerings launched. In their book *The Knowing-Doing Gap*, Bob Sutton and Jeff Pfeffer describe the many ways that organizations fail to translate what they "know" into action and progress. If you've ever taught before, you'll know that you really don't know a topic until you can teach it. The same is true for all of these ingredients. As touched on above, **make sharing what you've learned an essential part of your job responsibilities**.

Stay humble and stay open as you make the rounds sharing in the organization. I like to use the phrase "we want to share what we've seen..." as it keeps the dialogue open and focuses on what you've learned through your action. Don't shy away from the "obvious" truths that "we all know" and try to put a spotlight on your discoveries, especially those informed by customer feedback and evidence. When you communicate your findings with stakeholders and colleagues you open the door to knowing more, to updating your understanding later on by getting more evidence, and building credibility. That's why sharing evidence is essential.

ACTIVITIES

Jot down the top five customer problems you're seeking to solve with innovation. Take the top three and refine them. (I like to use mind-maps to help deconstruct and show the interconnections and components of a problem. Need-finding and customer discovery books will have a lot of good techniques to use too.)

Examine your assumptions, then identify the riskiest ones and find ways to efficiently validate them.

» What would have to be true to get the impact we want? To grow? To really win with new customers? To be wildly successful as a business?

» What assumptions, if proven untrue or impossible to act on, would sink our strategy or our offering or our business?

Consider a range of strategic options.

» How might you deliver the experience or interaction: What if it were digital? What if it were a service interaction? What if you licensed this? Worked with distributors? Delivered it directly?

» How might customers buy your offering: What if they subscribed to it? Leased it? Got to use it for free?

RESPONSIBILITY 5: GIVE GREAT FEEDBACK

Feedback, and its creative cousin, critique, is a skill that's hard to learn. Nonetheless, **giving great feedback keeps teams motivated and wanting to work on tough and uncertain problems**. Doing it poorly can often do more harm than good. While progress is the ultimate measure of innovation and customers are the ultimate arbiter of that progress, some feedback along the way from the innovation leader will help cultivate the ingredients we talked about in Responsibility #4.

Art and design programs practice a traditional form of "studio critique," so there might be skilled practitioners in your organization to watch and study. If not, here are some principles and techniques to help you deliver better innovation feedback today—because it can't wait.

BE CONSISTENT

Develop a consistent playbook of questions. Use the ingredients in Responsibility #4 as a roadmap for what to look for and have a set of go-to prompts for discussion.

If you have a tendency to wander or you have team members that do too, you can easily find yourself at a level of detail or in a part of the problem that's less pressing or important. If your approach is consistent, it will help the team prepare to have a discussion with you. It also demonstrates that what you care about is progress, that your interests aren't as important as good outcomes.

GO TO THEM

Don't wait for scheduled meetings to see how your team is doing. As we said in Responsibility #3, you want to free them up to do the work. Showing up and going to them is a strong signal of support. You're literally there to help.

Being in the project room also allows you to play detective and check for signs of dysfunction: what does their workspace look like? If Post-its cover every surface they may be stalled in brainstorming and need a nudge toward prototyping and feedback. Have they "solved" the problem too quickly, settling on one option without researching them all? Then it's time to slow them down and remind them not to play favorites yet.

BE DELIBERATE ABOUT TIMING

Be proactive and thoughtful about when and how you interact with teams. You might schedule feedback sessions (a good idea). Also poke your head in and check informally on their progress. If they're not there hopefully they're with customers or testing prototypes or building a new prototype to share soon.

Avoid giving tough feedback on Fridays. If possible, I like to go deeper on Tuesday mornings (Monday is fraught) and help the team think about ways to "win the week." Getting involved earlier in a project and even earlier in a given week helps prevent your team from feeling like they've wasted time or effort. I learned the idea of showing up earlier from Paul Bennett, the chief creative officer of IDEO, when I was there. If you show up with lots of great feedback, new ideas, or existential questions towards the end of the project, it can really demotivate a team. This is what's sometimes knowingly referred to as the "swoop and poop." Swooping and pooping is not very leaderly.

BE PREPARED

Don't wing it. Check in before a meeting to touch base on status, progress, and review any assets, stories, evidence, or outputs the team can share. Make sure you're ready and able to give good feedback. Be in a good mood—positive and optimistic, well-rested, well-fed, and not annoyed. Great feedback delivered with bad tone is worse than the bad ideas it purports to fix. Give yourself a ten-minute break before you go into the room to get yourself in a positive, helpful frame of mind.

My former colleague at IDEO Leslie Witt is now Head of Design for Intuit's 200-person Small Business Design Group. Leslie is a delightful teammate and accomplished leader. As she said in a recent interview:

"Don't undervalue the power of a smile. I know that
might seem ridiculously tactical, but tone matters
immensely and if people feel you're on their side
and that you're invested in them—which can come
through body language, through just literally seeing the
enthusiasm on your face—they're much more open to
considering the feedback."

SEPARATE PEOPLE FROM IDEAS

If you give feedback that separates the ideas from the people, and
help people be clear about their assumptions, you'll be able to have
better conversations and protect feelings. Creativity is a deeply
personal and vulnerable act. Feelings can be hurt. I've heard that
an extremely innovative CEO tells employees that while their
idea is not a good one (or even bad), they are "absolutely the right
person to be working on this problem." It may not be your style, but
there's something very powerful about the sentiment.

Today there's a tendency to fetishize "failure." Why? People
feel hemmed in at their jobs, they're uncomfortable being wrong,
and they want to avoid blame. If we put failure on a pedestal we
can focus on that rather than address the conditions that cause
people to avoid blame. At my consulting company, our business is
premised in part on the assumption that being wrong quickly and
efficiently is a better way to develop better solutions. The trick is
to get team members comfortable with the idea that we're doing it
on purpose and to use how we're wrong to make what we do next
(tomorrow) better.

HELP THE TEAM HAVE DISCUSSIONS WITH EACH OTHER

Have teams surface differences in assumptions and beliefs, then
mediate disagreements through the lens of evidence. Innovation
is most often a team pursuit. Be wary of taking sides, since the

customer or market is the ultimate arbiter anyway. Explore why your team is interested in a particular direction by being curious without being too Socratic (think *inquiry*).

If the team has differences of opinions, encourage them to quickly play that out through research or a quick prototype—the answer is "out there" rather than "in here." A team I was working with on a financial services project debated—it seemed for hours—about whether or not "fun" and "personal finances" might coexist in an interesting way. I encouraged them to make quick prototypes and put them in front of customers in our next round of research. Doing that took less time and got the team to more interesting answers than an internal debate ever could.

REMEMBER TO KEEP THE OPTIONS DISTINCT

Avoid collapsing and combining ideas too early. In Responsibility #4, we discussed the inherent value of distinct options. These often get collapsed in team reviews and feedback settings. Problem solvers want to solve the problem. We all want to get to an answer. Try to resist that impulse and help the team do that too. Explicitly invite them to separate and simplify their ideas. Work on making each option stronger and even have naysayers strengthen the idea they are least excited about. If you're choosing to move forward with an idea or option, I'd rather be choosing from the strongest set possible rather than a Franken-idea or ideas that could benefit from a little bit of improvement.

DO NO HARM

Sometimes the best feedback is no feedback. Instead, give positive reinforcement and encouragement to try something quickly. If you point out a problem, suggest ideas for how to solve it. This is described as "if you close a door, give them another door to open."

Back to Frank Hauser, the director mentioned in Responsibility #3. One of my favorite quotes from the book is #70 of his list of rules: "*Please, PLEASE be decisive.*" Too many leaders answer questions with "yes, no, or maybe." But maybe is confusing and demoralizing. It puts the team in limbo without offering a way forward. Obviously not all questions can be answered yes or no though, so instead of maybe Hauser reminds us that it's perfectly acceptable for leaders to admit "I don't know." Not only does "I don't know" convey humility and an openness to learning but it suggests next steps: where can you find that knowledge? And after all, as Hauser points out, you can always change your mind.

If "I don't know" is a good answer, "yes" is even better. Gordon MacKenzie, the "Creative Paradox" at Hallmark Cards, admits that he said yes to every idea that was brought to him. Every. Single. One. For *three years*. Good ideas and the people motivated to pursue them are most likely to make progress. So there's less harm in reinforcing the motivation than stamping it out.

ACTIVITIES

Get your team in one room to discuss:
» What kind of feedback is most helpful right now? What feels like the most important customer problem?
» What have you discovered? What's surprising? What's missing?
» What options for direction do you have? What are you trying next? What do you want to let go of for the moment?

RESPONSIBILITY 6: INSPIRE PROGRESS

A CEO recently told me "I wish I weren't the only person coming up with ideas." I hear that all the time. It often leads CEOs to grab for a process, but as we've seen, the problem goes beyond process. Uninspired and unmotivated people won't make any process successful.

Paradoxically, one way to inspire your team is to **stop coming up with ideas** and instead do the things we've been talking about in this book: frame problems, highlight assumptions, set a pace, and provide your team with time and resources to translate insights into ideas and ideas into launches. It won't happen overnight, of course, but it's worth working on. In the meantime, here are some more tips.

BE INSPIRED YOURSELF

Demonstrate the doing. Entrepreneurial founders often find ways to continue to spend time near and with their customers, even long after starting their company. You'll often see these executives eschew the CEO role to instead take a chief customer or chief product role. At some large companies they find ways to integrate staying close to the customers as well. Well-known examples are the way Southwest and Jetblue employees spend time working the front line at the airport and on flights. Similarly, A.G. Lafley, the CEO of Proctor & Gamble during a time of great growth and innovation, used to go out on customer visits with IDEO teams alongside other executives. IDEO and companies like it really led a revolution over the last thirty years by getting top leaders in their organizations to start from a place of inspiration. "Founder-led" or "designer-led" companies today are starting from that place of customer intimacy.

FIND INSPIRED PEOPLE

Look for and hire people who know how to inspire themselves. If a team member wants to be "inspired" it's not your job responsibility to transform and motivate that person. You might choose to work on it with them for other reasons, but their lack of inspiration and motivation can come from myriad places—and even though it's good to care about your people I don't think you can necessarily change their whole mindset. Innovation is fun work, but it's also hard. It might not be the right work for some people. Or they might have run out of steam. That happens too. Sometimes a change of perspective or a change of approach is needed for them and sometimes your teams need a fresh infusion of motivation, talent, diversity, and perspective. Innovation, for many, isn't a "forever job" so encourage some movement in the ranks. Look for people who inspire themselves all the time and be one of those people yourself.

MAKE INSPIRATION ROUTINE

Help your team to find that inspiration and try to make the activity routine by getting out, by interacting with other experiences/brands/ services, or by bringing in examples of experiences, products, and business models that you find stimulating. Tim Riley, the Director of Digital Experience at Warby Parker, hosted lunches on Fridays where team members would regularly bring in something they had heard or seen to talk about together. Anything. They didn't have to overthink it. It didn't have to be directly relevant. It just had to be interesting to them. Having that routine on the calendar encourages you to be looking for interesting things and it gets you in the practice of being able to describe why it's interesting to you.

NUDGE

Use time and money to get teams moving. Sometimes even inspired teams or individuals need a little kick-start. For example, people may have ideas of what to explore that they keep bringing up, but things stop at the idea stage. Teams that are further along in a process might find themselves stalled with indecision about which path to follow next. I like to look for opportunities to give a nudge—a reminder of what they're interested in—paired with a check, or a limited amount of time, money, or other resources to help them take the first or next step. You might offer design help, a different set of eyes for feedback, or one of those deadlines that help get them back into the world to do some research or prototyping. Help people get unstuck and they might come back to you when they find themselves stuck again.

STEP AWAY FROM THE PROBLEM

Help everyone take a step back. In businesses today, there's an epidemic of burnout compounded by busyness masquerading as forward motion. At the same, there have been studies that show how important and creative boredom can be.

One underappreciated (and boring!) activity in an innovation project is just cleaning things up. Clark Scheffy, another former colleague at IDEO, once told me "everybody likes to look at their wood pile." There's something comforting in surrounding ourselves with all the work we've done: Post-its, old prototypes, presentation drafts, etc. Search Google for "innovation project rooms" and you'll find images of glass-walled rooms plastered with a rainbow of Post-its. They should clean those rooms up more often! You can take pictures of all of it, so go ahead and do that and recycle the physical proof. Force yourself to edit and hold on to the most important artifacts of your work.

At the marketing software company Percolate one of the things they do is put versions of their web pages in frames on their wall. If you want to know what Percolate "is" you can open up a browser or just as easily walk over to the wall and see what's launched and out there.

GO HOME

If all else fails, help your teams get away, hit pause, and just do something else. I like to remind teams that the "weekend doesn't start itself."

ACTIVITIES

» Go on a field trip with your team. Pick a place that's interesting and go there and talk about what was interesting about it.

» Try a "clean room" session: Go with the whole team to a clean room and tell the story of your project. Then talk about what's most interesting and exciting about what you're doing.

» Go visit a team that needs a break. Find a way to get them to take that break.

RESPONSIBILITY 7: REWARD PROGRESS

When I was working with *The New York Times* on several new digital product projects David Perpich, who led what was then called NYT Beta, stopped me in the hall one day. It was budget review season and he was collecting input on what projects should be prioritized for funding. "Ryan, how would you decide what to fund next?" With little else to go on, my answer was still pretty easy. "Fund what's growing. And if you aren't in a position of growth yet, give resources to the teams getting traction and making the most progress." **As an innovation leader you are in a position to control and allocate resources so reward the people and projects making progress**. The corollary is that you should starve inaction.

Clients new to innovation usually ask some variation of the question: "How do you know what's working?" You'll want to see visible and concrete examples of what the Lean Startup and customer discovery people call "validated learning." Look for better and clearer "ingredients" for innovation, like problem statements, customer insights, assumptions, options, and evidence, as discussed in Responsibility #4. Whether it's part of the "official process" or not, as an innovation leader, you need to find ways to make that happen.

ALLOCATE RESOURCES CAREFULLY AND SHELVE WHAT'S NOT PROGRESSING

It's okay to pause projects that aren't advancing. Maybe you don't have the right team to move it forward. Maybe the market isn't ready. Maybe there are other efforts that are getting more traction. Maybe we can't overcome a certain technical challenge without adding capabilities first (and do we want to do that?) Shelving projects is not the same as killing them off. Change is going to happen and you never know when conditions will make that idea ripen. Shelving them is a way of acknowledging that it won't work for now, but it might sometime, and you can always restart them. If you stay lean, you'll give yourself that option. If you're aligned on the customers and problems (yes, you've fallen in love with the problem), I suspect you'll be back to tackle it again someday soon.

Staged funding and capping work-in-progress is the best way to allocate resources. Different types of innovation options benefit from different types of funding. Eric Ries' latest book, *The Startup Way*, is a good place to look for guidance here as is Rita Gunther McGrath's work on innovation portfolio types and financial forecasting for innovation.

DON'T ACCEPT IDEAS AS A FINISHED PRODUCT

Insist upon seeing some progress and action in exchange for more resources. In *The Lean Startup*, Eric Ries tells the story of SnapTax, an Intuit innovation. A small team has a radical idea, identifies the most critical assumptions, gets just enough funding to test them, solves for them, gets more funding, rinse, and repeat. That's the way to do it.

The alternative is becoming responsible for the "idea suggestion box." It's become a cliche in many organizations that ideas can and should come from "anywhere." Often this is coupled with idea jams or the rollout of idea management software. Some people describe this as "innovation theater." Ideas, especially poorly articulated, can easily become your responsibility. It sounds counter-intuitive, but you should know by now that **innovation is not solely about ideas**. Try not to get saddled with them as your job.

If you do, it's likely you'll be looking at a sea of similar-sounding, oft-heard ideas of wildly different magnitude and priority. What often happens next is that employees end up saying, "look, I gave them my idea and they did nothing with it. This place isn't serious about innovation and entrepreneurship." Worse than before. As an innovation leader, you want to take responsibility for evidence, progress, and outcomes, not potential starting points.

DON'T WASTE ENERGY ON SKEPTICISM

You may find yourself in a crowded room talking about innovation in organizations, hearing front-line innovation stories, debating how or if innovation can happen when people in the organizations don't have the skills, and debating the top problems we should be trying to solve as our businesses are under assault from all manner of market, technological, and societal changes....

You know what's coming. At some point, a few people may start asking "what do we even mean by innovation?" or "isn't innovation just jargon anyway?" or "should we even be talking about innovation when _____ is happening?" Snickering. Knowing glances. All that.

Get away from those people.

Let me pose a different set of questions: are you interested in business growth? In solving new customer problems? In launching new offerings? In finding a way to keep your business relevant, growing, and important in the future? If these answers are "yes," then you're interested in innovation.

If you do find yourself in charge of innovation and surrounded by skeptics, consider whether you should be there and, if so, what that means for your approach and how you'll sidestep, co-opt, or address the skeptics. The more you feel like you have to convince your leaders, the less likely success will be.

SET YOURSELF UP TO BE SUCCESSFUL

Demonstrate progress in order to build credibility and get support. Focus. Think big and act small. Rolling out a company-wide innovation process is neither focused nor small. You already know I don't think that's your job. Developing a new set of potential offerings for a priority customer segment is hard enough and represents true progress.

Progress is satisfying in and of itself. As an innovator, you're setting out to make new things for customers to make their lives more fulfilling, interesting, better, safer, or easier. As an innovation leader, you get to amplify that feeling by working and supporting others. And that, to me, is the most rewarding work of all. I wish you all the progress in the world.

CITATIONS

This book either cites directly or draws upon the following sources.
For a complete guide to what and who to read and why, see
http://makingprogressbook.com

Ackoff, Russell. Interview with Glenn Detrick (2011).
http://gdetrick.org/2011/12/08/an-interview-with-russell-l-ackoff/

Amabile, Teresa. *The Progress Principle* (2011).

Blank, Steve. *Four Steps to the Epiphany* (2013).

Constable, Giff. *Talking to Humans* (2014).

Cummings, Keenan. "A Working Definition of Product Design."
Medium. June 5, 2013. https://medium.com/@keenancummings
/a-working-definition-of-product-design-4e48069727c8

Gothelf, Jeff and Josh Seiden. *Sense and Respond: How Successful
Organizations Listen to Customers and Create New Products
Continuously* (2017).

Hauser, Frank. *Notes on Directing: 130 Lessons on Leadership from
the Director's Chair* (2008).

Jacoby, Ryan. "Innovation Measures" blog posts. *Do_matic*
(October 2009).

Knight Foundation. "Developing Clarity: Innovating in Library
Systems." March 30, 2017. https://knightfoundation.org/reports
/developing-clarity-innovating-in-library-systems

MacKenzie, Gordon. *Orbiting the Giant Hairball: A Corporate
Fool's Guide to Surviving with Grace* (1998).

McGrath, Rita Gunther. *Discovery-Driven Growth* (2008) and
The End of Competitive Advantage (2013).

Muoio, Anna. "How Is Your Company Like a Giant Hairball?" An interview with Gordon MacKenzie. *Fast Company* (December 31, 1997). https://www.fastcompany.com/32950 /how-your-company-giant-hairball

Pfeffer, Jeffrey and Robert Sutton. *The Knowing-Doing Gap: How Smart Companies Turn Knowledge into Action* (2000).

Portigal, Steve. *Interviewing Users: How to Uncover Compelling Insights* (2013).

Ries, Eric. *The Lean Startup* (2011) and *The Startup Way* (2017).

Selden, Larry and Ian MacMillan. *Manage Customer-centric Innovation Systematically.* (April 2006) https://hbr.org/2006/04 /manage-customer-centric-innovation-systematically

Witt, Leslie. Interview (August 15, 2017). https://www.invisionapp.com/blog /inside-design-intuit/

ACKNOWLEDGMENTS

First, thanks to Josh Seiden, Jeff Gothelf, and Vicky Olsen at Sense & Respond Press. Josh has been a collaborator in practice and a mentor in spirit and when he said, you should write a book, I was just scared enough to want to try it.

Much of what I try to do in this mini-book is to bring together useful principles and ideas from my experiences doing projects and studying innovation, design, and entrepreneurship. That would be impossible without the decades of practice and research done by others, especially practitioner-friendly researchers and experts. Rita McGrath and Bob Sutton stand out. They each disavow originality, even while being original and, best of all, kind.

My colleagues at IDEO for seven years in Palo Alto and New York taught me so much about design, innovation, product design, and creativity in many forms. I'd especially like to acknowledge all of the people in the project rooms who let me work with them and I did a poor job of leading. I wish I had done more of this with you when we were together then and there. I'd like to thank Tom Eich, Victoria Lubomski, Alix Zacharias, Clark Scheffy, Colin Raney, Mimi Chun, Diego Rodriquez, Tim Brown, John Ravitch, Paul Bennett, and Dave Strong. IDEO introduced me to Anese Cavanaugh, a wonderful leadership coach when I was there. She's been instrumental in any of my successes since then.

To start a new company and to have any of that success, it's really less about the chances you take and more about the chances others take on you. My clients at MACHINE over the last six years have been as trusting as they are ambitious and inspired, especially Jennifer Hsieh, Todd Cleary, Ann Schultz, Jodi Kahn, Russell MacClemore, Gwen Sullivan, Maura Shea, Catherine Sun, John Bracken, Gene Han, Ali Heron, Aron Pilhofer, Alex Wright, Kari Wilson, Cordy Swope, Amy Foley, David Perpich, Alex MacCallum, and Ben French. My collaborators at MACHINE have been what have allowed us to really pressure-test ways to make progress. I'd especially like to thank the talented and patient Janvi Jhaveri, Maria Norelli, Kevin Shaw, Mimi Chun,

Rachelle DiGregorio, Leigh Mignona, and Liz Seibert Turow for being as professional as they are talented.

My formal love for problem-defining started at the University of Virginia, in the amazing Systems Engineering department, it evolved at Deloitte Consulting under mentors like Steve Martin and Brian Caplan, and it blossomed alongside my classmates at Stanford Business School and under the guiding tutelage of the founding team and early professors at what is now the Stanford d.school, especially Jim Patell and David Kelley. They made it ok for me to make crappy prototypes and feel ok being weird doing it. My students and colleagues at the School of Visual Arts Interaction Design Program in New York City remind me that I really don't know anything about the past and even less about the future.

Finally and most importantly, my wife Stephanie, an inspiring marketing leader, and Henry, an accomplished toddler leader, are my motivation and daily inspiration. To my parents Allyn and Cynthia (now gone), they made it ok for problems to be problems, solutions to be engineered, and for me to become me. Thank you.

RYAN JACOBY is the founder of MACHINE, a strategy and innovation company that helps innovation leaders at clients like The New York Times, Google, Marriott, Nike, Viacom, and Feeding America "Think Big and Act Small." Prior to MACHINE, Ryan led the New York office at the design and innovation firm IDEO, where he built the Business Design discipline. In some circles, he's known as the "first graduate" of the Stanford d.school.

www.machine.io
🐦 @jacobyryan

Made in the USA
Monee, IL
04 February 2020